Horses!

Horse Riding

Sara Louise Kras

Cavendish Square

New York

Published in 2014 by Cavendish Square Publishing, LLC
303 Park Avenue South, Suite 1247, New York, NY 10010

CPSIA Compliance Information: Batch #WS13CSQ

All websites were available and accurate when this book was sent to press.

Library of Congress Cataloging-in-Publication Data

Kras, Sara Louise.
Horse riding / Sara Louise Kras.
          p. cm.— (Horses!)
 Includes bibliographical references and index.
 Summary: "Provides comprehensive information on basic horse riding, English style, and Western style"—Provided by publisher.
 ISBN 978-1-60870-837-6 (hardcover)   ISBN 978-1-62712-087-6 (paperback)   ISBN 978-1-60870-843-7 (ebook)
 1. Horsemanship—Juvenile literature. I. Title. II. Series.
SF309.2.K73 2013
798.2'3—DC23
2011029917

Editor: Christine Florie
Art Director: Anahid Hamparian
Series Designer: Virginia Pope

Expert reader: Cathy Herbert, former director of publications, American Horse Shows Association

Photo research by Marybeth Kavanagh

Cover photo by John P. Kelly/Image Bank/Getty Images

The photographs in this book are used by permission and through the courtesy of: *Getty Images*: Universal History Archive, 4; Kate Connell/Photographer's Choice, 18; David Handley/Dorling Kindersley, 20; Apic, 28; Visions of America/Joe Sohm/Image Bank, 41; *Landov*: Rusty Costanza/The Times-Picayune, 6; *Alamy*: Mary Evans Picture Library, 7; North Wind Picture Archives, 8; John Terence Turner, 10; Manfred Grebler, 17; Ken Welsh, 21; RIA Novosti, 26; vario images GmbH & Co.KG, 29; Kumar Sriskandan, 31; Luc Novovitch, 34; *SuperStock*: Robert Harding Picture Library, 13, 37; F1 ONLINE, 14; Belinda Images, 33; *Photo Edit Inc.*: Kayte M. Deioma, 16; *Photolibrary*: Peter Arnold, 24; *Newscom*: Chuck Haney/Danita Delimont Photography, 38

Printed in the United States of America

Contents

One

Why Ride Horses?

People have ridden horses for thousands of years. No one knows exactly when or how people first **domesticated** and rode horses. We do know that humans were aware of the existence of horses as early as 30,000 BCE. This is because **archaeologists** have discovered ancient cave drawings of horses, among other animals.

But it wasn't until thousands of years later that humans and horses developed a bond. Experts believe that humans began riding horses around five thousand years ago on the steppes, or wide-open plains, of Asia.

Since that time, people have ridden horses for traveling and hunting. During medieval times in Europe, soldiers rode horses into the battlefield. People also entertained ancient kings and nobility with horseback sports such as jousting and horse racing. Today, the sport of horse racing continues. Racetracks can be found in many cities on most continents. Expert riders

← The Bayeux Tapestry, circa 1067, depicts an Englishman hunting atop his horse. Horses played a role in how the early English worked, traveled, and fought.

A Jockey's Life

Rosie Napravnik is a famous jockey. Napravnik said, "Being a jockey is exciting because I have the drive to win. I love the horses and the competition. I have ridden horses my whole life—since the age of two. When I was seven years old I was in a **Pony Club**. We had races, which I won while riding a Welsh mountain pony."

Sometimes jockeys have to race horses that they have never ridden. To help a jockey understand a horse's personality before a race, horse and rider sometimes do a drill called breezing. To breeze a horse, the jockey rides at high speeds to see how the horse might do in a race and to learn the horse's habits.

Jockeys often travel a lot from state to state in order to compete at racetracks or fairgrounds. They may stay in one location for two to eight months at a time while racing.

Even though Napravnik rides horses for a living and travels most of the time, she owns a horse at home. Rosie's horse is named Sugar, and it lives with Rosie's mom. When Rosie is in town, she rides Sugar just for fun. They ride on trails, go jumping, and even go swimming together.

called jockeys are paid to race some of the fastest horses in the world.

Riding Styles

As horses became more important in daily life, people began to observe them and their natural motions. Around 2,500 years ago, a Greek horse trainer named Xenophon became famous for his close observations of horses. He used his studies to teach riders how to give horses subtle cues to change their movements. Together, rider and horse could quickly turn, charge, step sideways, or stop. Through this method, the rider and horse became as one. This type of training was very useful on the battlefield, and it was the beginning of English-style riding.

Ancient Greek soldiers learned the fine art of horsemanship, which proved helpful on the battlefield.

About five hundred years ago, another horseback riding style began to appear. This type of riding, which started in Spain and Portugal, came

A vaquero steers his horse with one hand and swings a lasso with the other.

to South America with the Spanish conquistadors. They introduced cattle-working and warfare practices that are the foundation of today's western-style riding. Spanish cowboys, called vaqueros, used **saddles** and **bridles** different from the ones used in English riding.

Vaqueros had to move herds of cattle long distances. They sometimes had to catch a steer or cow while trying to control their horses at the same time. Their riding style allowed them to keep both reins in one hand, while the other was free to **lasso** a wandering cow.

One of the most common reasons to ride a horse today is for pleasure. It's a great way to enjoy nature, to get exercise, and to make friends with other riders. But for some horseback riders, there's more to it than that. They feel freedom, power, and a sense of adventure when exploring acres of land on horseback. Many riders feel like they are flying when they jump. While galloping, they feel like the wind.

Two

Basic Horseback Riding

Horseback riding has changed over time, but one thing has remained the same: new riders still have to learn the basics. First you have to get on the horse, and then you have to steer it. You'll need to tell it to go, to change direction, to speed up, or to stop. How do you give a horse all these commands? It may seem confusing, but with a good instructor, you will learn to ride correctly.

Instructors generally work at riding schools. You can find a riding school through a friend, a local veterinarian, your local Pony Club, or even a **tack** shop—a store that sells saddles, bridles, and other riding gear. There may be many riding schools, informally called barns or stables, in your area. Before choosing one, visit several. While visiting them, try to answer the following questions:

← Receiving riding lessons from a professional trainer
can get a beginner off to a good start.

- Are the horses healthy, happy, and well cared for?
- Do they have water in their stalls?
- Are their stalls clean?
- Does the barn have friendly staff?
- Do they staff members have experience?
- Do they answer your questions?
- Are the other riders enjoying the barn?

After you've decided on a riding school, it's time to go on your first ride.

In the Saddle

Before you can get in the saddle, you'll first need to approach the horse to become acquainted. Because horses are big, this process can be a little bit scary. Your instructor will help. Walk toward the horse from the front, but slightly to the side. A horse's eyes are on the side of its head, so it cannot see straight ahead very well. If it doesn't see what is walking toward it, the horse can become frightened. A horse cannot see directly behind its body, so never approach one suddenly near its back legs. The horse could become startled and kick. When you are next to the horse, let it sniff your hand. Then pet the horse gently on the side of its neck with a smooth motion.

After you're acquainted with the horse, it's time to get on. Always **mount** the horse on its the left-hand side. Hold the reins loosely in your left hand, and rest your hand on the horn or **pommel**, which is at the front of the saddle. Put your left foot into the **stirrup**. Push up with both feet, swing your right leg across the saddle, and sit gently. Position your feet in the stirrups so that your heels are pointing down. The ball of each foot should rest in the stirrup. Now, take the reins in each hand, or in one if your are riding western style. It's time to start giving the horse commands.

Riders mount from the left side of the horse.

Why Mount on the Left Side?

There are many explanations for why horses are mounted on the left-hand side. The most likely reason is that soldiers and knights used to carry long swords on their left-hand side. After putting on their horse's saddle and bridle on the left side, it was easiest to mount the horse on the left. A soldier would swing his right leg over the horse's back. His sword was free to hang on the left side without harming his horse.

Steering the Horse

To communicate with the horse, you can use your legs, hands, and voice. You should always be gentle, relaxed, and exact, so that the horse understands your commands. Give the horse one or two light, short squeezes with both

How Do the Reins Work?

The reins are connected to a headpiece called a bridle (below). The bridle is made of leather straps and usually has a metal piece called a **bit**. The bit is placed in the horse's mouth and is used to control the horse. All bits should be smooth so that they do not hurt the horse's mouth.

The bit helps the rider give the horse instructions by applying pressure in the horse's mouth. It's important to choose the right type of bit, so the horse feels only pressure, not pain. Bits differ by the horse. Some horses need more encouragement to do as the rider commands. Other horses may need more sensation from the bit to follow commands. Riders should always be gentle with the reins so the horse doesn't have pain from the bit.

legs to ask it to walk. The horse's head nods as it walks. Stay relaxed and let your legs and hands move slightly with the motion of the horse.

Steering a horse is similar to steering a bicycle. To turn left, look in the direction you want to go. This will automatically shift your weight. Also, apply a little light pressure with your right calf against your horse's side. If you're holding the reins with two hands, move both reins to the left just a little. If you're riding western with one hand, your horse will turn left when it feels the rein against the right side of its neck.

Sitting Properly

During your first few horseback riding lessons, you may not steer a horse much at all. Instead, you will learn how to sit on a horse. This is called having a good seat. Having a good seat helps you to stay balanced. It helps the horse, too, because it enables the horse to understand your instructions more clearly. In addition, a good seat prevents strain on the horse's back.

While practicing your seat, the trainer either holds a lead rope and walks along beside you or attaches the horse to a long rope or **lunge line** and then stands in the middle while the horse walks in a circle. Your instructor will show you how to use your hands, legs, and seat independently. Various exercises will help you improve your balance in the saddle. Experienced riders know that having a good seat looks natural. To have a good seat, you should be centered in the saddle. While sitting in the saddle, imagine a straight line drawn from your ear to your shoulder to your hip and to your heel. If someone were looking at you from any angle, you would be sitting perfectly straight.

An instructor holds a lunge line during lessons at an equestrian center.

Changing Gaits

After you've practiced sitting correctly and steering your horse, your instructor will have you change the horse's **gait**. There are four main gaits. In English riding they are called walking, trotting, cantering, and galloping. In western style they are called walking, jogging, loping, and galloping.

To change gaits from walking to trotting, nudge the horse gently with your calves. The horse will start to trot. A trotting motion is not smooth. Instead, you will move up and down along with the horse.

Cantering is faster than trotting. To get the horse to speed up into a canter, stop moving with the trot. When you are firmly in the saddle, gently nudge the horse's side with your calf. Keep your upper body and hands in place.

The gallop is the fastest. Before you command your horse to gallop, make sure you are comfortable with walking, trotting, and cantering. Horses can get excited when they start gaining speed. To tell your horse to gallop,

The fastest gait for a horse is the gallop.

incline your upper body a little forward and squeeze with your outside leg. When changing gaits, you can also make a little clucking or kissing sound.

To stop the horse, press your legs lightly against the horse's sides, pull the reins back firmly, and then release. If the horse doesn't respond the first time, pull the reins back a bit more firmly and then release. You can also add the verbal command "Whoa."

There are many steps in learning to ride. It will take time and lots of practice. Trusting your trainer and your horse will help. As you become more familiar with your horse and the commands, horseback riding will become more natural.

Three

Rider and Horse Bond

Learning to ride at a riding school is a great way to start. To better understand your horse and to develop a bond, some schools require that you **groom** and **tack up** your horse before riding. As time goes by, you may start to notice your horse's behavior and moods. This is especially true if you are riding the same horse each time or if you own a horse.

If you do plan on owning a horse, you will soon discover that it is a huge responsibility and a lot of hard work. Horses are not the same type of pet as a cat or a dog. They must be ridden and looked after daily. But horse owners feel it is worth the work because of the strong connection, even love, that develops between them and their horses. Some owners described their horses as having human qualities such as generosity, honesty, and courage.

← Many horse owners and riders develop a strong bond with their horse.

Before the Ride

When going on your first ride, you should expect that a saddle and bridle will be on the horse. This step is usually done for you if you're going on a short trail ride. If you are taking horseback riding lessons, you will probably learn to do this yourself.

The saddle and bridle are not put on the horse until the dirt has been brushed off of the animal and its hooves have been cleaned. Grooming your horse before a ride is a way to become acquainted. You may find places where your horse is especially sensitive—and they may be similar to spots where you are ticklish. While brushing your horse, you should also look for any cuts or scratches. If your horse has an injury, even if it's small, you should let your instructor know. That way your horse can get medical attention from a veterinarian if needed.

When your horse's coat is smooth and shiny, it's time to put on the saddle and bridle. Gently place the saddle on a blanket or pad. The **girth** fastens the saddle to the horse. It hangs from the saddle on the right-hand side. Then the

Before riding, spend time grooming your horse.

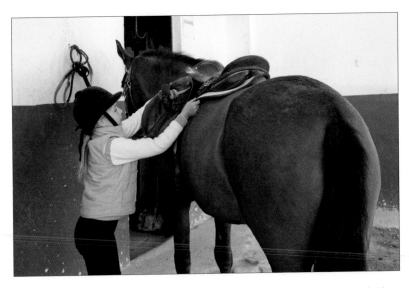

Before riding, it is important to place the saddle securely on a horse's back.

girth strap is pulled under the belly of the horse and then buckled on the left side of the saddle. This is the most important step. Check the girth several times, especially before you mount the horse, to make sure it's tight enough. If the girth is too loose, the

A Horse's Cleaning Kit

A **currycomb** (a stiff, round comb), a stiff brush, a softer brush, and a **hoof pick** make up a horse's cleaning kit. The currycomb first removes mud and loose hair. The stiff brush removes the remaining loose hair and dirt. The soft brush is then used to clean and shine the horse's coat. Always pay extra attention to the area where the saddle is placed. If there is dirt between the horse and the saddle, sores may form.

The hoof pick removes loose rocks and dirt, especially around the **frog**, a sensitive region of the hoof. It's very important to keep a horse's hooves clean. A stuck rock can bruise its foot.

saddle could slip sideways while you are on the horse's back. The last thing any rider wants to do is fall off a horse because of a loose girth. It is not only embarrassing, but also very dangerous.

After the saddle is securely on, the bridle is placed on the horse's head. The bridle helps the rider control the horse.

What Does a Horse Think?

Tacking up a horse is a useful way to become familiar with it. But after spending many hours with the same horse, you may start to wonder what is on your horse's mind. One of the most important things to understand about horses is that they are prey animals, similar to zebras in Africa. This has been the case since almost a million years ago. Before horses and humans became friends, horses were hunted by predators. This fact alone explains why horses act in certain ways. Loud noises and sudden movements frighten horses because they could mean a predator is near. Horses are constantly watching out for predators. That is why they sleep standing up—so they can make a quick escape.

Horses do not like to be alone. They prefer to be able to see other horses at all times. To horses this means survival, because a herd protects them from predators. In nature, one of the horses in the herd becomes the leader. The other horses follow the leader.

When riding a horse, you must let the horse know that you are the leader. The way to do this is to know exactly what you want the horse to do. Then you must lead the horse. Horses can tell if a rider is nervous and confused or if a rider knows what he or she is doing. If the horse begins to doubt that you are the leader, it will stop doing what you're telling it to do. If you tell the horse to do something and it resists, make the command again. It may take some patience, but you must get the horse to follow your command. The best riders are confident riders who are consistent about their commands. Make sure to make commands the same way every time so that you do not confuse the horse.

How to Approach a Sleeping Horse

Because horses sleep standing up, it's hard to tell if your horse is asleep or just standing. The way to tell if a horse is sleeping is to look at its back legs. If one leg is bent with the top of its hoof resting on the ground, it is asleep. If you need to approach a sleeping horse, make some noise—not too loud, but loud enough for the horse to hear you—so it won't become startled.

Horses have a language all their own. A horse's ears, mouth, and body position can give you clues. If you understand this language, it will help you guide your horse. When a horse's ears are pointed forward, it is interested in what is happening and is paying attention to it, not to you. If one of the horse's ears is turned slightly to the side, or if its ears are moving a little to the side, it is paying attention to you. If both of the horse's ears are laid back, the horse is hurt or angry. When you see this, especially if you are in the horse's stall, you should stand away from the horse. It may kick or bite.

Sometimes a horse curls back its upper lip. It may look like the horse is making a face, but what it's really trying to do is to get a strong sniff of an odor it doesn't know. This action, called flemming, pulls air into the top of its mouth, where it has special scent organs. This helps the horse to figure out what the smell is. When a horse licks its lips, it may be expecting food.

Horses curl back their upper lip when trying to identify an unfamiliar scent.

How to Give a Horse a Treat

After going on a horseback ride, it's fun to spoil your horse and give it a treat. Horses love carrots and apples. You might want to chop the carrot or apple into bite-size pieces to make it easier to feed it to the horse.

To give your horse a treat, calmly and slowly approach it. Place the treat in your palm and hold it under the horse's muzzle. Keep all your fingers flat, especially your thumb, so they don't get nipped by mistake. The horse will gently take the treat with its front teeth.

You will find that the more time you spend with horses, the better you'll understand them. Even though horses are large animals, they are gentle and patient. Many experienced riders have learned successful ways to treat a horse. You should always be calm and patient. Correct your horse firmly and lovingly. Never jerk its mouth, hit its head, or whip it. When tacking up, be careful around your horse. Make sure you know where its feet are so that it won't step on you. After all, the horse weighs ten to twenty times more than you do! That's why it's such a fantastic feeling when a horse does what you ask.

Four

English Style

If you've decided to learn to ride English style, you will soon discover that it is all about speed, control, and elegant horsemanship. This is achieved through slight shifts by the rider in the saddle and reins, which are held softly. Today, English style is taught all over the world. This style is used in competitions such as **dressage**, jumping, racing, and polo.

English Style's Long History

English riding has a long history. About 2,500 years ago, Xenophon, a Greek horse trainer, wrote a book that presented horseback riding as an art form. Xenophon's ideas were the beginning of English style. As time passed, European horse trainers further developed the style.

← A rider and horse participate in a dressage competiton.

Federico Grisone, an Italian, was one of these Europeans. He wrote a book about horseback riding in 1550. This book's instruction included Greek riding methods, as well as strategies for riding in medieval battles. Grisone opened a riding school in Naples, Italy, where rulers and kings learned how to ride a horse properly.

Grisone also taught horses how to perform tricky movements. This advanced style, called dressage, was more of a show rather than practical horseback riding. Grisone taught horses to rear up on their hind legs and to do other interesting stunts. His training method was sometimes cruel, however. This would change in the early 1600s with riding master Antoine de Pluvinel.

De Pluvinel taught King Louis XIII of France how to ride. He also showed that horses could be taught amazing feats through patience and praise. His ideas proved successful. Through de Pluvinel's methods, even today, horses stay happier and live longer.

These early horse trainers observed horses and their natural movements. They then taught horses to make their natural movements on the rider's command.

King Louis XIII of France receives a riding lesson from Antoine de Pluvinel.

The Spanish Riding School

The Spanish Riding School of Vienna, Austria, was established 430 years ago. The school received its name because of the Spanish-bred Lipizzan horses that trained there. Later, these horses with flowing manes and tails were sold throughout Europe.

The showy Lipizzan horses are still taught how to perform beautiful movements. Some of these movements are gallops. The horses perform a prancing gallop, a gallop in line with other horses, a gallop in place while turning on their hind legs, and a slow gallop. They can also rear up on their back legs, hop on their back legs, and jump high into the air and kick out their legs. They complete all of these movements with a rider in the saddle, and it is truly art in motion. Today, these charming horses entertain people from all over the world at the Spanish Riding School. Performances are given many times throughout the year. Lipizzan horses also go on worldwide tours.

The rider gave these commands with subtle cues in the saddle, such as slight shifts in the legs, hips, seat, and upper body. In addition, the rider held the reins softly and gave the horse constant, subtle instructions with the bit.

As time went by, these methods became more advanced. Horses were taught to perform difficult stunts such as leaping into the air, marching in place without moving forward, and other acrobatics. The movements look almost like ballet. This style of horseback riding is still taught today at the Spanish Riding School in Vienna.

English Style Today

English style has developed over thousands of years to what it is today. To steer the horse in English style, hold a rein firmly in each hand. Then use both reins to steer the horse. Your arms should be bent, but there should be a straight line from your elbow to the horse's mouth to foster clear communication.

Another lesson you will learn in English style is how to post the trot. When your horse begins to trot, you will move up and down with the horse's motion. To do this, you let the horse's movement lift you up and forward in the saddle while keeping your legs still and your hands steady.

During your lessons, you will learn to ride on a basic English-style saddle, which is small and light. An English saddle has a pommel in the front and saddle flaps on each side. Different types of English saddles are used for competitions such as dressage or jumping.

English Gear

In either English or western style, a good helmet is one of the most important pieces of riding gear, especially for a new rider. A riding helmet protects your head in case you fall off the horse. Riding helmets are similar to bicycle helmets. They are hard on the outside and have padding on the inside. The helmet must fit your head correctly to protect it, so an expert should help you purchase one.

English-style boots are tall and tight and have a smooth sole with a heel. Riders wear pants called **jodhpurs**. These closely fitted pants are especially designed for horseback riding. They are made with knee patches or a full leather seat. This protects the knees from rubbing against the horse's sides, so the pants last longer and the rider doesn't have chafed legs.

If you are competing in a riding event or playing a sport such as polo, there may be a special outfit for it. You might need a special shirt, jacket, or vest for competition. For sports, you might need a uniform.

Competition

English-style riding competitions began when soldiers rode on horseback. In cavalry training, soldiers had to learn many horseback riding skills. Today, two common traditional English-style competitions, which were part of the old cavalry training, are dressage and jumping. During these competitions, riders show off their skills and compete against each other.

Dressage competitions are performed in an arena. The rider gives the horse subtle cues to perform different movements. The judges score the rider and the horse on how well they work together and how well the horse performs the gaits.

In jumping, the rider and horse canter around a course with eight or more fences that they must jump. Sometimes fences include a small pond

English-Style Sport

Polo is a sport played on horseback. The teams ride English style and use long, wooden mallets to hit a wooden ball. The object of the game is to get the ball down the field and hit it through the goal posts at the end. Polo is very popular in England. The British royal family has played polo for almost a hundred years.

Jumping is one event in an English riding competition.

or mimic a brick wall or a big hedge. If the horse doesn't make it over the fence, the rider-and-horse team receives a penalty. Jumping competitions also have penalties for taking too much time.

English-style horseback riding is done throughout the world. This elegant type of riding can be watched during the Summer Olympics.

Five

Western Style

The western riding style developed for practical reasons. Its history comes from cattle ranching in Europe. It began more than five hundred years ago, when the Spanish conquistadors came to the New World.

Beginners learning western riding will soon find out that this style is all about comfort. The western saddle is sturdy and wide. It was designed to be comfortable for cowboys who spent all day on horseback. This saddle gives the rider the ability to move around as needed, for roping, sorting, and herding cattle. The front of the saddle has a horn to which the rider can tie a cow that's been roped. The reins are held in one hand, and the grip is much looser than that of English style.

Today there are many western-style competitions throughout the United States. During many of these competitions, riders and horses perform movements that cowboys still use when they herd cows today.

← Western style riding can be seen at rodeos, competitions, farms, and ranches.

The First Cowboys

Western style started with the vaqueros, the original cowboys. These Spanish herdsmen brought their traditions with them to the New World in the late 1400s. In addition to bringing horses to the Americas, the Spanish introduced long-horned cattle.

The first cattle ranchers lived in Mexico. These ranchers hired vaqueros to ride on long cattle drives from New Mexico or Texas to Mexico City. The cattle were then sold to the highest bidder.

Later, cattle ranches were established in other western states. Cattle drives became common, as a way to move cattle from rural areas to towns to sell. Cowboys drove up to three thousand head of cattle long distances, and the process sometimes took a couple of months.

On the trail, cowboys faced many dangers. Western riders often had to have one hand free to shoot intruders or to lasso a wandering cow. Because the reins were held in one hand, the other hand was free to swing the rope into the air to catch the cow.

Today, western-style horses are still steered with one hand, with the reins held thumb up. The rider's entire arm, from shoulder to wrist, moves the reins to steer the horse. If you are right-handed, you hold the reins in your left hand. This leaves your right hand free for roping or other activities.

Western riders use neck reining to control their horses. In this type of reining, the horse responds to the pressure of the rein against its neck.

A cowboy rides his horse in the western style: one hand holding the reins, the other holding a lasso.

The horse then moves in the opposite direction, away from the pressure.

While on the trail, western riders became highly skilled at steering their horses and lassoing animals. When in towns, cowboys competed in roping skills, reining skills, and many other contests. These competitions still occur today in western riding events and at rodeos.

Western Gear

Western riding gear is all about being practical. Hanging from the sturdy saddle are long, wide stirrups. The long stirrup straps allow cowboys to stretch out their legs while riding. The wide stirrups spread out the pressure of the foot and give cowboys room to move in the saddle.

A cowboy's clothing is also useful. Leather **chaps** are used to cover jeans or other pants to protect them while riding. Cowboy hats have wide brims to protect the eyes and face from the sun. Cowboy boots have pointed toes and heels, perfect for fitting and staying in the stirrup.

Western gear is not only practical, but also often decorative. It is common to see designs etched into the leather of the tack or small metal plates attached to saddles and fenders.

Western Competitions

Western horse shows and rodeos have many competitive events. Most of them have to do with cattle ranching. One of the competitions is reining, which has become an international sport. Reining is western style's form of dressage. The rider has to steer the horse in different patterns that follow the types of footwork used on a ranch. Two of these patterns are spins and sliding stops with a rollback. The horse spins by turning its front legs, one crossing in front of the other. Meanwhile, the inside hind foot, called the pivot foot, stays in place. Spins are used on the ranch when a horse has to turn quickly to control a cow's movement.

In the sliding stop, a horse gallops down the arena and builds speed. The rider says "Whoa" while adjusting his or her legs and body. The horse then brings its hind legs underneath while locking the joints and slides. Dust flies into the air as the horse slides 20 to 30 feet. At the end of the sliding stop, the horse hesitates, then lifts its front end and does a rollback, or turns so that its facing the direction from which it came. Then the horse lopes off quietly in the other direction. This mimics what a horse would do when chasing a cow.

Out on the Trail

Trail events are also part of western-style competition. The rider-and-horse team must complete a pattern that features challenges such as closed gates,

Trail Ride Rules

To stay safe on the trail, you need to follow certain rules. The most important rule is to wear a helmet at all times. Only lope and gallop when the trail is clear far ahead. When passing farm animals, always keep your horse at a walk, and leave the animals alone. Take care not to frighten them. Stick to the trail, and don't wander away from the group. If a gate is opened, close it after you go through.

bridges, and poles that have to be crossed. Sometimes the horse needs to move backward or sideways to get past the challenges. The rider and horse are timed and scored on how well they handle each challenge.

Trail rides through open fields, mountain trails, or city park trails are also done for pleasure. During these types of rides, there is no competition. It's just a great time to bond with your horse.

Pleasure trail rides can be either western style or English style. But for long rides and overnight trips, western style is more common. Horseback riding camps in the mountains usually follow western style. Ranches sometimes offer summer western-style programs for visitors who want to see what it's like to be a cowboy.

No matter the style, riding allows you to enjoy the outdoors, get exercise, and bond with your horse.

Whichever riding style you choose, after you become familiar with horses and understand them, you'll soon discover what amazing creatures they are. Even though most people do not need horses to get from place to place, riding a horse just makes it more fun.

Glossary

archaeologist   A person who studies artifacts from the past.

bit   A metal bar put in a horse's mouth to help steer and control it.

bridles   Leather straps and metal pieces put on a horse's head so the rider can steer it.

chaps   Open leather pants worn over trousers to protect riders from bushes and chafing.

currycomb   A comb that has rows of ridges used to clean a horse's coat.

domesticated   To be tamed.

dressage   A style of riding in which the rider communicates through slight movements.

frog   The fleshy area on the sole of a horse's hoof.

gait   A type of running or walking.

girth   A band that goes under the horse's belly and holds a saddle in place.

groom   To brush and clean a horse.

hoof pick   A curved metal tool used to clean a horse's hoof.

jodhpurs   Riding pants that fit tightly at the knees and ankles.

lasso   To use a long rope with a loop to catch a cow or other animal.

lunge line   A long rope attached to a bridle that is used to exercise a horse in a circle.

mount   To get up on a horse.

pommel   The highest part of the front of a saddle.

Pony Club   An organization that educates young people about horses and riding.

saddles   Leather seat made for horseback riding.

stirrup   A ring with a flat bottom, hung by straps on a saddle. This is where a rider puts his or her foot.

tack   The saddle, bridle, and other equipment used to ride a horse.

tack up   To prepare a horse for riding by putting on all the equipment.

Find Out More

Books

Gray, Susan. *Horse Shows*. New York: Cavendish Square, 2014.

Ransford, Sandy. *The Kingfisher Illustrated Horse and Pony Encyclopedia*. Boston: Kingfisher, 2010.

Trueit, Trudi Strain. *Horse Care*. New York: Cavendish Square, 2014.

Wilsdon, Christina. *For Horse-Crazy Girls Only: Everything You Want to Know about Horses*. New York: Feiwel and Friends, 2010.

DVDs

Introduction to Horseback Riding and Horse Care. Paramount Home Video.

Ride Like a Natural: Sitting Right on Your Horse. Trafalgar Square Publishing.

Websites

Horseback Riding Camps

www.kidscamps.com/sports/horse.html

On this website, young horse riders can find a summer camp near them.

U.S. Pony Club

www.ponyclub.org/

Become a member of the Pony Club and find a local club center. Students can also learn about horse competitions and upcoming events.

Index

Page numbers in **boldface** are illustrations.

About the Author

Sara Louise Kras has ridden horses since she was a little girl. Because she was raised in small towns, horses were always around. She has done a lot of western-style trail riding. When she was a teenager, she went to a horse camp, where she rode in the mountains of Colorado. As an adult, she went to a horse camp in the Sierra Nevada in California. Her favorite thing while riding horses is to gallop and feel the wind in her hair.

Kras grew up in rural areas of Washington state, Texas, and Colorado. She has always loved the outdoors. She currently lives in Glendale, California, with her husband and cat. Kras is the author of more than thirty books for children.